Level 1

Series editor: Philip Prowse

Inspector Logan

Richard MacAndrew

CAMBRIDGE
UNIVERSITY PRESS

CAMBRIDGE UNIVERSITY PRESS
Cambridge, New York, Melbourne, Madrid, Cape Town,
Singapore, São Paulo, Delhi, Tokyo, Mexico City

Cambridge University Press
The Edinburgh Building, Cambridge CB2 8RU, UK

www.cambridge.org
Information on this title: www.cambridge.org/9780521750806

First published 2002
13th printing 2011

Printed in the United Kingdom at the University Press, Cambridge

A catalogue record for this publication is available from the British Library

ISBN 978-0-521-75080-6 Paperback
ISBN 978-0-521-68637-2 Book with Audio CD Pack

Richard MacAndrew has asserted his right to be identified as the Author of
the Work in accordance with the Copyright, Design and Patents Act 1988.

Illustrations by Debbie Hinks

Contents

People in the story

Inspector Jenny Logan: a police officer in Edinburgh
Sergeant Grant: an officer helping Inspector Logan
Robert Kerr: a man living at Royal Terrace
Margaret Kerr: Robert Kerr's wife
Andrew Buchan: a doctor
Sergeant McCoist: a police officer in North Berwick
Tommy: a ten-year-old boy
Lizzie: Tommy's older sister

Places in the story

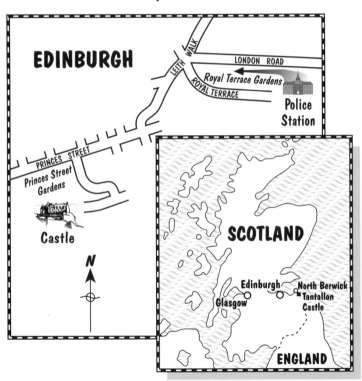

Chapter 1 *Where is Margaret Kerr?*

'When did your wife go out?' asked Jenny Logan. She looked at the man across the table from her. He was tall with dark brown hair.

'Yesterday,' he replied. 'At lunchtime, I think. I wasn't at home at the time. I went out just after twelve and got back about two.'

'And she didn't come home last night?' said Logan.

'That's right,' said the man.

'Is she often out all night?' asked Logan.

'No,' said the man. 'Never.'

Jenny Logan sat back in her chair and looked at the man. It was a cold Monday afternoon in April and it was her first day in her new job. She was an inspector in the

Edinburgh police – a new job in a new city. Sergeant Grant sat on her right. He had a pen and some paper. Logan looked at Grant.

'Your name, sir?' Grant asked the man.

'Robert Kerr.'

'Your wife's name?'

'Margaret.'

'And where do you live?' asked Grant.

'On Royal Terrace,' replied the man. Royal Terrace was a pretty street that looked down across the Royal Terrace Gardens to the police station on London Road. Kerr told Grant the number of the building and the flat, and Grant wrote it on the paper.

'And your wife left your flat about lunchtime yesterday afternoon and she still isn't home?' Grant made it a question.

'That's right,' said Kerr.

Grant wrote on the paper.

'What clothes did she have on?' asked Logan.

Kerr thought for a minute. His eyes looked up over Logan's head.

'A white pullover and a black skirt,' he said. 'And a dark red coat. She had a brooch on the front of the coat.'

'What kind of brooch?' asked Logan.

'It's a big brooch. A flower,' replied Kerr. 'But I don't know what kind. Just a flower.'

Logan looked at Grant, then turned back to Kerr.

'Do you have a photo of your wife?' asked Logan.

Kerr took out a small photograph and put it on the table. Logan looked at it. Margaret Kerr had long blonde hair and blue eyes. She looked happy in the photo.

There was a brooch on her blouse in the photo. It was a flower.

'Is that the brooch?' asked Logan.

Kerr looked at the photo.

'Oh yes,' he said. 'That's it. I didn't know it was in that photo.'

'How old is the photo?' asked Logan.

'About a year, I think,' replied Kerr.

Logan looked at the photo again. Then she looked at Kerr. 'Is everything OK at home?' she asked. 'Is there anything wrong? Is your wife unhappy?'

'No,' said Kerr quickly. 'No. We're very happy.'

'Is she with friends? Or with family?'

'No,' said Kerr. 'Nobody knows where she is.'

Logan looked at Kerr and thought for a minute or two.

'The thing is,' she said, 'I can't do very much. Your wife isn't a child. She can go away for a few days – I can't stop her. And I can't ask my officers to try and find her because . . . well, she's not a child.'

'Oh!' Robert Kerr looked a little unhappy.

'I can put her photo in tomorrow's newspaper,' she said.

'Yes. OK,' said Kerr. 'Thank you.'

'Maybe somebody knows where she is,' said Logan.

*   *   *

Half an hour later Logan and Grant sat in Logan's new office. Logan had short brown hair, brown eyes and she wore a blue suit. Grant wore an old blue jacket and some old black trousers.

'What did you think of Mr Kerr?' asked Logan.

Grant thought for a minute and looked at his new inspector. He didn't know much about her. Maybe she was good, maybe not.

'I don't know,' he said. 'Why?'

Logan looked at Grant and then out of the window.

'I don't know,' she said. 'I feel something's not right. But I don't know what.'

Grant said nothing. Logan gave him the photograph of Margaret Kerr. 'I'd like this photo in tomorrow's papers. Can you do that?'

'No problem,' said Grant, and he stood up and left the room.

Logan watched him leave. She thought it was unusual that Grant did not call her 'madam'. Sergeants usually call inspectors 'sir' or 'madam'. Was it her age? He must be about fifty-five and she was only twenty-six. Or maybe he just didn't like new inspectors. Anyway, she thought, right now it wasn't important.

Chapter 2   *What did Tommy see?*

At nine-thirty on Tuesday morning, Logan was in her office at the London Road police station. The door opened and Sergeant Grant came in. A young boy and a woman came into the room behind him. The boy was about ten years old with red hair and blue eyes. The woman was about nineteen or twenty years old, too young to be the boy's mother. She had long black hair and all her clothes were black.

'This is Tommy Burns,' said Grant, putting his hand on the young boy's back, 'and his sister, Lizzie.' He turned to Tommy. 'This is Inspector Logan.' Then he looked at Logan again and said, 'Tommy's got something to tell you.'

'Go on, Tommy,' said Lizzie from behind Sergeant Grant. 'Tell the inspector. Tell her what you saw.'

Logan stood up and came out from behind her desk.

'Miss Burns,' she said to Lizzie, 'please sit down.' She turned to Tommy 'You too, Tommy.' Then Logan sat on the front of her desk and looked at them. Lizzie opened her mouth to speak but Logan put up a hand and stopped her.

'Miss Burns,' she said, 'your brother has something to tell me. I'd like to hear it from him.' Lizzie closed her mouth.

'I saw her,' said Tommy.

'Saw who?' asked Logan.

'The woman in the paper. That woman,' said Tommy, looking at Logan's desk. On Logan's desk was the morning paper with a photograph of Margaret Kerr on the front.

'OK, Tommy,' began Logan, 'when did you see her?'

'On Sunday afternoon. About one o'clock.'

'Where was this?' asked Logan.

'On Princes Street,' replied Tommy. Princes Street is Edinburgh's big shopping street.

'Are you sure about the day and the time?' asked Logan.

'Of course,' said Tommy. 'I always meet my friends in the Princes Street Gardens on Sunday mornings, and we go back home for lunch about one o'clock.'

Logan said nothing. She just waited. Tommy spoke again. 'Anyway, I went into a shop to buy a drink and that woman pushed into me. And she didn't say sorry. That's why I know it was her.' Tommy looked at the photo again.

'So you had a good look at her?' asked Logan.

'Yes, I did,' said Tommy. 'She didn't say sorry. I was angry with her.'

Logan smiled. 'I can understand that,' she said. 'So tell me about her. What did she have on? Did she have a coat on? Or a hat?'

Tommy closed his eyes and thought for a minute or two. Then he spoke: 'She had a red coat on. A kind of dark red. No hat. She was wearing a black skirt and black shoes.' He stopped for a minute and then said, 'And a white pullover under her coat. I could just see that.'

'Are you sure about all that?' asked Logan.

Tommy looked at Logan. 'I didn't have my eyes closed,' he said.

Logan smiled again. 'Anything else? Think about it.'

'No,' said Tommy.

Logan sat back and looked out of the window and thought for a minute. She looked at Tommy again.

'Was the woman happy?' she asked. 'Or sad?'

'I don't know,' Tommy replied.

'What did she do?' Logan asked.

'She got into a car. And they drove away.'

'They?' asked Logan.

'She wasn't the driver,' said Tommy. 'There was a man in the car too. He was the driver.'

'What about him?' asked Logan. 'Did you see him?'

'No. The car was too far away.' Tommy didn't have answers to all their questions. He began to look sad.

'What about the car?' asked Grant.

'I don't know,' said Tommy. He looked down. 'I'm sorry. I don't know anything about cars. It was blue. That's all I know.' He looked at his shoes and did not look up.

'It's OK, Tommy,' said Logan, putting a hand on his arm. 'Thank you for coming and talking to us.'

Tommy looked up at Logan and smiled.

Tommy and Lizzie Burns left the room and the phone rang. Logan answered it.

'Inspector Logan,' she said. She listened for a minute and said only 'OK' and 'Right'. Then she said, 'Do you want to come here? . . . OK, see you in half an hour.' She put the phone down and looked at Grant.

'That was Sergeant McCoist from the North Berwick police. They found Margaret Kerr this morning,' she said. 'She's dead.'

Chapter 3 *A name on Margaret Kerr's phone*

Half an hour later Sergeant McCoist sat in Logan's office with Logan and Sergeant Grant.

'We found the body at Tantallon Castle,' said Sergeant McCoist.

Tantallon Castle is an old castle by the sea about forty kilometres east of Edinburgh, near the town of North Berwick.

'How did she die?' asked Logan.

'Someone hit her on the head,' said McCoist.

'What did they hit her with?' asked Logan.

'We don't know,' said McCoist. 'We've got twenty-five officers looking round the castle now.'

Logan said nothing.

'We found her bag,' McCoist said, 'so we knew who she was. And her photograph was in this morning's paper, so I called you.'

'Thank you,' said Logan.

'There was nothing very interesting in her bag,' said McCoist. 'Some letters from her family, money, credit cards. But this is hers,' he put his hand in his jacket 'and maybe there's something here.' He took out a mobile phone and put it on the desk in front of Logan. Logan took the phone and looked at it. Then she looked at McCoist.

'Did she have a red coat on?'

'Yes,' said McCoist.

'And a brooch on the coat?' asked Logan.

'Pardon?' said McCoist. He didn't understand.

'A brooch,' said Logan again. 'Was there a brooch on the coat?'

'No,' said McCoist. 'Why?'

'Well, she had one on when she left home on Sunday,'

said Logan. 'Anyway, thank you for the phone. Maybe you're right. Maybe there's something here.'

McCoist left and Logan played with the phone for a minute. 'That's interesting,' she said. 'Her last call was to an Andrew Buchan. I'd like to know who he is.' She looked at Grant. 'We need to talk to Robert Kerr . . . to tell him that his wife is dead.' She gave Grant the phone. 'Ask someone to find out who this Andrew Buchan is, and where he lives. Then meet me at my car.'

*   *   *

Logan and Grant stood at the front door of Robert Kerr's flat on Royal Terrace. It was twelve o'clock.

Kerr answered the door. He wore a light blue pullover and brown trousers.

'Could we come in for a minute, sir?' asked Logan. Kerr stood back and Logan and Grant walked in.

The living room was big but warm with lots of red and brown colours. There was a table with a telephone on it. Next to the telephone there were business cards from restaurants, a hotel, taxi companies and a card from a car rental company. Kerr and Logan sat down. Grant stood by the door and watched.

'My wife?' asked Kerr.

'I'm sorry,' said Logan.

Kerr's eyes opened wide.

'I'm sorry,' said Logan again. 'We found her body this morning at Tantallon Castle.'

'How . . .?' began Kerr, but he stopped. Then he began again. 'How did she . . .?'

'Someone killed her,' said Logan.

'Oh no!' said Kerr. His hands went up to his face. Logan watched him.

'Mr Kerr,' she said, 'I know this is a bad time, but I do have some questions.'

Kerr put his hands down. 'Please, Inspector, ask your questions. Any questions.'

'Do you know someone called Andrew Buchan?' asked Logan.

There was no noise in the room at all. Kerr looked at Logan, then at Grant, then back to Logan.

'Yes, Inspector,' he said. 'I know Andrew Buchan. Well, I know who he is, but I don't know him very well. He's a doctor, I think. He lives just down the road.'

'On Royal Terrace?' asked Logan.

'Yes.'

'What number?'

'I don't know,' replied Kerr. 'Down to the left. A red front door. I don't know the number. But why are you asking about him?'

'We think that maybe he can help us,' said Logan. She didn't want to talk to Kerr about Andrew Buchan now. 'Do you have a car?' she asked.

'No,' said Kerr.

'But you can drive?' asked Grant from near the door.

'Yes, I can drive,' said Kerr, 'but I don't have a car.'

Just then Logan's phone rang. She answered it and said 'Yes', 'Thirty-six', 'OK' and 'Thank you', then put the phone back in her bag.

She looked at Kerr. 'Andrew Buchan lives at number thirty-six,' she said. 'And we need to speak to him. Once again I'm very sorry about your wife, and thank you for your time.'

Chapter 4 *Dr Andrew Buchan*

Logan and Grant stood at the front door of 36 Royal Terrace, not far from Robert and Margaret Kerr's flat. A short man in a grey jacket and trousers and a red tie answered the door.

'Andrew Buchan?' asked Logan.

'Yes.'

'I'm Inspector Logan of the Edinburgh police and this is Sergeant Grant. I understand you know a Mrs Margaret Kerr?'

Buchan looked at Logan but didn't say anything. Then, very slowly and quietly he said, 'Yes. Yes, I do. But how do you know?'

'We'd like to come in and ask you some questions about her.'

Andrew Buchan's living room looked out over the garden at the back of his house. Logan and Buchan sat in chairs by the window. Grant stood near the door.

'So, how do you know Margaret Kerr?' asked Logan.

Buchan looked out of the window and said nothing for a minute or two. Then he turned to Logan.

'We were lovers,' he said slowly. 'I loved her very much. And I thought she loved me.'

'You *thought* she loved you?' asked Logan.

'Yes,' said Buchan. 'But it's over. She finished with me last week. Last Saturday.'

'Finished with you?' asked Logan 'Why?'

Buchan looked out of the window again. 'I wanted her to leave her husband and live with me. She didn't want that. So she finished with me.'

Logan looked at Buchan but did not speak. Buchan put his head in his hands.

'I didn't understand. She doesn't love her husband. She doesn't *like* her husband. But she doesn't want to leave him.' Buchan looked up again. 'I asked her again and again to leave him. I wanted her to be my wife. Then on Saturday I said to her, "You must leave Robert or we're finished." And she said, "OK, Andrew. I'm sorry, but then we're finished." And she left.'

Buchan put his head in his hands again.

'Did you see her after Saturday?' asked Logan.

'No,' said Buchan.

'Do you have a car, Dr Buchan?' asked Logan.

'Of course.' Buchan looked up quickly. 'I'm a doctor. I need a car for my work.'

'What colour is it?' Grant asked.

'Blue. Why are you asking all these questions?'

Logan sat back and looked at him.

'I'm sorry, Dr Buchan,' she said. 'We found Margaret Kerr's body at Tantallon Castle this morning. Someone killed her. I'd like you to come to the London Road police station with us.'

Buchan's face turned white and his hand went up to his mouth. 'Oh no!' He thought for a minute, then he spoke again: 'You didn't answer my question – how did you know about us?'

'Her phone,' said Logan, and she stood up. 'She called you on Sunday. Get your coat, Dr Buchan.' Then Logan turned to Grant. 'Get some officers here to look round Dr Buchan's house. Maybe there's something interesting here.'

'OK,' said Grant.

Chapter 5 *Logan makes some phone calls*

From two o'clock to four o'clock Logan and Grant questioned Andrew Buchan in the London Road police station. Buchan told them he last saw Margaret Kerr on Saturday afternoon. He said he tried to call her on Saturday evening but there was no answer. Then she phoned him on Sunday morning and said he mustn't ring again. Buchan told Logan and Grant that he was at home all day on Sunday and didn't drive anywhere.

After two hours of questioning, Logan and Grant left Buchan in the room with a police officer. They went to Logan's office for a cup of tea.

'We need to look at everything,' Logan said. She drank some tea. 'What about Buchan's house? Did they find anything there?'

'I don't know,' said Grant. 'Do you want me to see?'

'Yes, please,' replied Logan, and Grant left the room.

Grant still didn't call her 'madam', but it was only her second day. 'He wants to see how good I am,' she thought.

Logan finished her tea. Grant came back. There was a smile on his face and a small bag in his hand. He put the bag on the desk in front of Logan. There was a brooch in the bag. A brooch like a flower.

'They found this at Buchan's house,' he said.

'Where?'

'In a rubbish bag at the front of the house,' said Grant. 'Tuesday is rubbish day on Royal Terrace. The officers saw

the bags out all down the street and had a look in Buchan's bag. There were all the usual things: old papers, bits of food, old teabags . . . and this.'

Logan took the brooch out of the bag and looked at it. On the back were some words and letters. They read 'To M with love from Andrew'. She put the brooch back in the bag and sat back in her chair.

'Did you see the back?' she asked.

'Yes,' said Grant. '"To M with love from Andrew".'

'Do you think Buchan killed Margaret Kerr?' Logan asked Grant.

'Maybe,' said Grant. 'Buchan wanted her to leave her husband but she didn't want to leave him. Buchan was angry. He drove her out to Tantallon Castle in his car – it is blue – killed her and left her body there. He took the brooch from her coat because it had his name on it. He didn't want the police to know he was Margaret's lover.'

Logan said nothing. She looked out of the window and thought for a minute. Then she turned to Grant. 'I don't like it,' she said.

'Pardon?' said Grant. He didn't understand.

'I don't like it,' Logan said again. 'I'm going to make some phone calls. Go and get Mr Kerr and bring him in. I want to talk to him again.'

Grant left and Logan got the phone book and opened it at car rental companies. She started making phone calls. Forty-five minutes later she was still on the phone when Grant came back. He heard some of her conversation.

'You're sure? . . . How far did he go?' Logan wrote something on some paper in front of her. 'Good. And is the car still with you? . . . What colour is it? . . . Good. Did it go out yesterday? . . . OK . . . Listen – nobody must go near the car. Some police scientists are going to come and look at it. OK? . . . About twenty minutes . . . OK. Thank you very much.'

Logan put the phone down and looked at Grant.

'Kerr?' she said.

'In the next room,' replied Grant. He looked questioningly at Logan but she just smiled and walked out of the room.

Chapter 6   *Logan finds the killer*

'Why am I here?' asked Kerr. 'I answered all your questions.'

'Yes, you did,' said Logan. 'But I'm not happy about one or two things.'

Kerr said nothing. He just looked at Logan. Logan and Grant looked back at him. The room was quiet.

Then Logan spoke: 'Andrew Buchan was your wife's lover,' she said.

'What?' said Kerr. 'Margaret! A lover?'

Logan stood up and began to walk round the room.

'Yes,' she said. 'Now think about this. Buchan loves your wife and he wants her to leave you. But she doesn't want to. He's angry. He doesn't want to live without her, but he can't have her. He doesn't want you to have her. He takes her out to Tantallon Castle and kills her. He leaves her body there. But there's a brooch on her coat. He gave her that brooch and on the back it says, "To M with love from Andrew". To Margaret from Andrew. Andrew Buchan, of course. So he takes the brooch. He doesn't want anyone to know about the two of them. And he puts the brooch in a rubbish bag in front of his house. Sadly for him, the police find it and, of course, the killer.'

'That brooch . . .' began Kerr. 'And Andrew Buchan . . . the killer? He killed my wife?'

'No,' said Logan.

'What?' asked Kerr.

Grant looked at Logan too. He didn't understand.

'Think again, Mr Kerr,' said Logan. 'Think again. A man wants to kill someone. He takes her out to Tantallon Castle and kills her. The dead woman has a brooch. A brooch with the man's name on it. Does he leave the brooch there or bring it back?'

'Well . . .' Kerr didn't know what to say.

'He brings it back,' said Logan, 'because he doesn't want anyone to see it. And where does he put it? In a bag in front of his house? Somewhere easy to find?' Logan stopped walking round the room and looked at Kerr.

'No,' she said. 'He doesn't put it there. That's stupid. And Dr Buchan is not stupid. He didn't put it in the bag in front of his house.'

'But . . .' Kerr tried to speak.

'I was never happy about the brooch.' Logan started walking again. 'A young boy saw your wife on Sunday afternoon in Princes Street, Mr Kerr. That boy got a very good look at her and he told us what clothes your wife had on. He remembered everything very well. But he didn't talk about the brooch. I thought a lot about that. Then I thought of this: how did you know your wife had the brooch on? You didn't see her leave the house on Sunday afternoon. You told us you were out.'

Kerr started to speak. 'But that's –'

Logan put up a hand.

'You're going to be sorry you told us about the brooch,' she said.

Kerr said nothing.

'So why did you want us to think your wife had the brooch on?' Logan said. 'And how did Andrew Buchan get the brooch and put it in his rubbish?' Logan sat down in front of Kerr.

'Do you want to know?' asked Logan. 'It's clever. He didn't put it there. You did.' Logan's face was centimetres away from Kerr's. 'You knew about your wife and Buchan.

You drove your wife to Tantallon Castle and killed her. You drove back and you waited. You wanted us to think Buchan was the killer. So you got your wife's brooch and put it in his rubbish. Very clever.'

Grant looked at Logan with wide eyes. Logan sat back in her chair.

'You wanted us to think that Buchan killed your wife and took the brooch because it had his name on it. But we questioned Andrew Buchan. He told us that your wife was his lover. He was happy to tell us. So, why did he take the brooch? Because he didn't want us to know about him and your wife? No. He told us everything.'

'This is stupid,' said Kerr. 'Anyway, I don't have a car.' There was a thin smile on his face.

Logan sat back. 'Ten minutes ago,' she said, 'I spoke to a nice young woman at Paterson's Cars on Leith Walk.' She looked at her watch. 'Our scientists are over there now. They're looking at a car. A blue car. The car they rented to

29

you on Sunday. They're going to find something, aren't they? One of Margaret's hairs, maybe? Maybe something from her coat?'

Kerr's face went white but he looked into Logan's eyes.

'Yes,' he said. 'You're right. I killed her. We were never happy. She slept with lots of men. Andrew Buchan was one of many. I didn't want to live with her any more. I hated her. I hated living with her. I wanted her dead. I killed her. And I'm happy about it.'

He sat back from the table and looked from Logan to Grant and back.

'Take him away, Sergeant,' said Logan.

'Yes, madam,' said Grant.

'Madam?' thought Logan. And she smiled.

Cambridge English Readers

Look out for these other titles in the series:

Level 1

Help! *by Philip Prowse*

Frank Wormold is a writer. To help him finish one of his stories he starts to use a computer. But the computer gives him more help than he wants. Then he really needs 'help'!

Just Like a Movie *by Sue Leather*

Brad Black goes to the movies every weekend with his girlfriend, Gina. They are happy, but have no money. Then Brad has an idea and thinks that real life can be just like a movie – and that's when things go wrong.

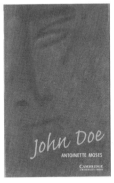

John Doe *by Antoinette Moses*

The man they call John Doe lies in a hospital bed. The doctor wants to know who he is. But John Doe doesn't answer his questions. When John Doe leaves the hospital, the doctor finds out more about him than just his real name.

The Big Picture *by Sue Leather*

Ken Harada takes photos for newspapers. But life gets dangerous when Ken takes a photo of a sumo star. Someone wants the photo badly. But who? And why?

Level 2

Logan's Choice
by Richard MacAndrew

'I'm Inspector Logan of the Edinburgh police,' Jenny said. 'I'm very sorry about the death of your husband.'

Who killed Alex Maclennan? His friend, his wife or her brother? It isn't easy, but Logan has to choose.

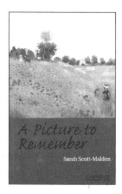

A Picture to Remember
by Sarah Scott-Malden

Cristina Rinaldi works for an art museum in Buenos Aires. One day she has a motorbike accident and can't remember some things. But there are two men who think she remembers too much, and they want to kill her before she tells the police what she saw.

The Double Bass Mystery
by Jeremy Harmer

Penny Wade is a musician. She goes to Barcelona with her orchestra. But her double bass is lost, and then someone in the orchestra dies. The police want to know what happened and Penny's life changes as she slowly learns the truth.

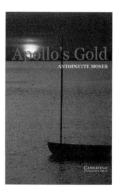

Apollo's Gold by Antoinette Moses

Liz studies and teaches archaeology in Athens. She goes on holiday to the beautiful and peaceful island of Sifnos. But the peace does not last long: a mysterious yacht arrives, one of the local men dies, and Liz becomes involved with some very dangerous people.